Elizabeth W. Greenleaf

C Is for Circus

BOOK 1

Notes from the Publisher

Composers in Focus is a series of original piano collections celebrating the creative artistry of contemporary composers. It is through the work of these composers that the piano teaching repertoire is enlarged and enhanced.

It is my hope that students, teachers, and all others who experience this music will be enriched and inspired.

Frank J. Hackinson

Frank J. Hackinson, Publisher

Notes from the Composer

Oh, when the circus comes to town
    I feel excitement rise;
I know I'll get a workout in my
    neck and in my eyes.
I look up high and then down low,
    I look from left to right;
The circus makes me concentrate,
    I cannot miss a sight.

This music that I wrote for you
    will keep you moving too,
For in a circus few stay put,
    there's just too much to do.
So let your hands shift up and down,
    and move them all around,
And play enthusiastically—
    the circus is in town!

D1413818

Elizabeth W. Greenleaf

Elizabeth W. Greenleaf

Contents

FF1160

It's Circus Time!

Hear the drums and trumpets of the circus parade!

Elizabeth W. Greenleaf

Teacher Duet: (Student plays 1 octave higher)

*Teacher pedals on duet.

Topsy-Turvy Tumblers

Imagine tumblers performing flips, rolls, handsprings, and cartwheels.

Teacher Duet: (Student plays 1 octave higher)

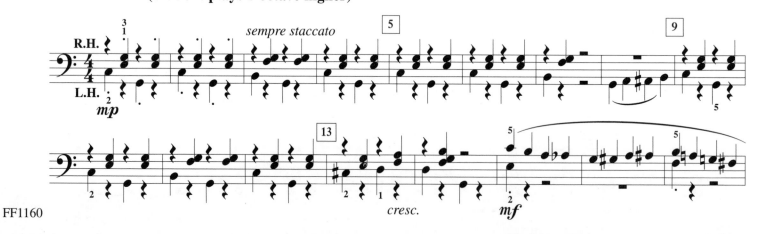

Waltz of the Wonderful Bears

The waltzing bears take three steps per measure. They move gracefully at a moderate speed.

Happy Jugglers

Play this piece with a relaxed, light touch, just like jugglers tossing balls.

11

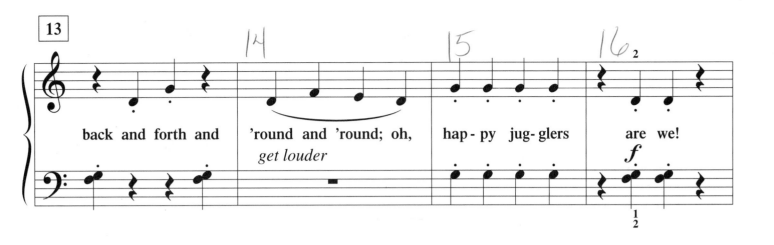

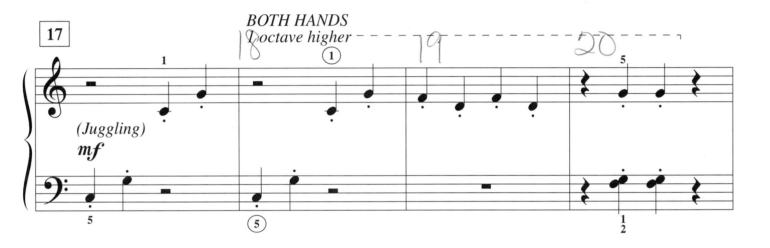

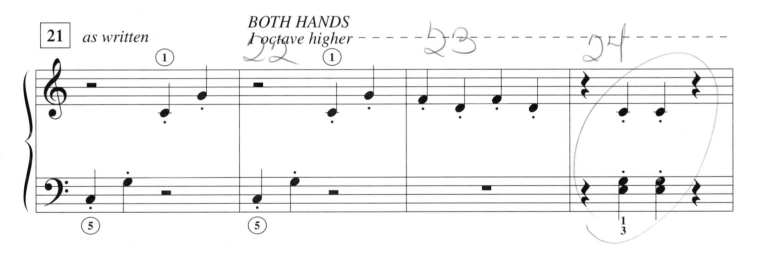

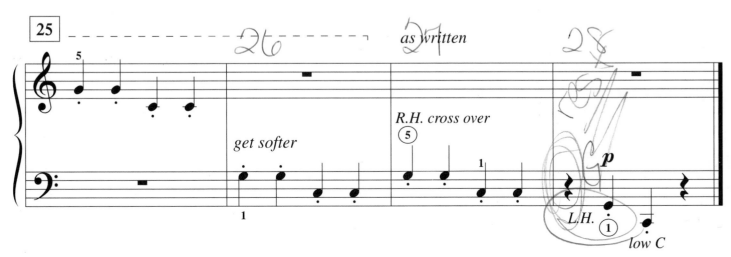

Acrobats Afloat

Let your hands float gracefully from one position to another,
like acrobats gliding from swing to swing.

Calmly flowing

2nd time R.H. 1 octave higher

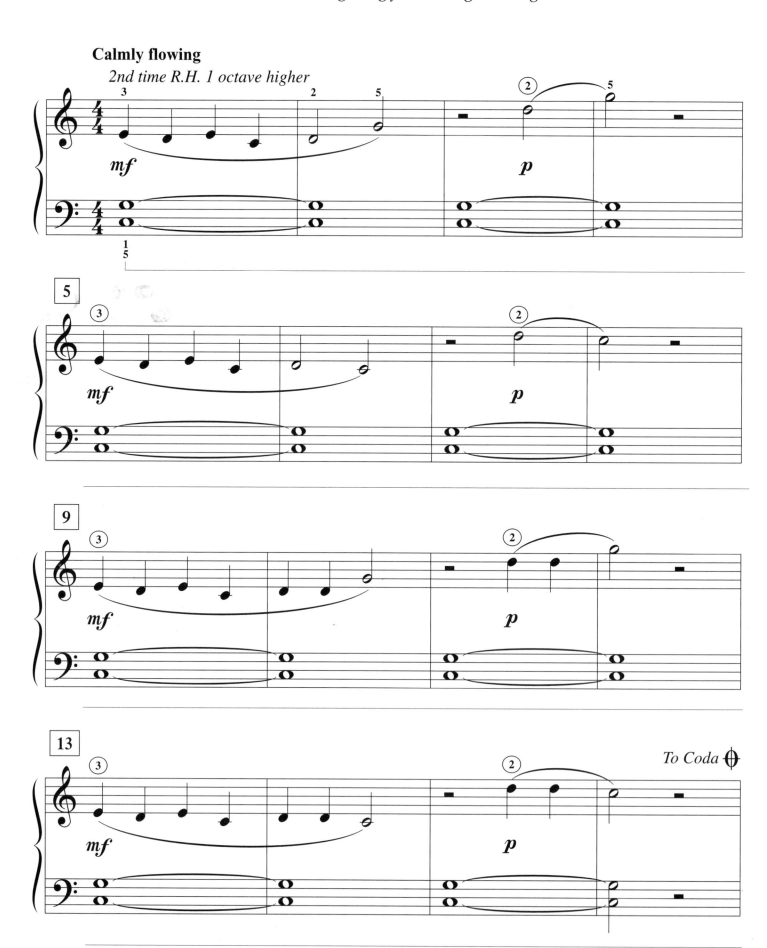

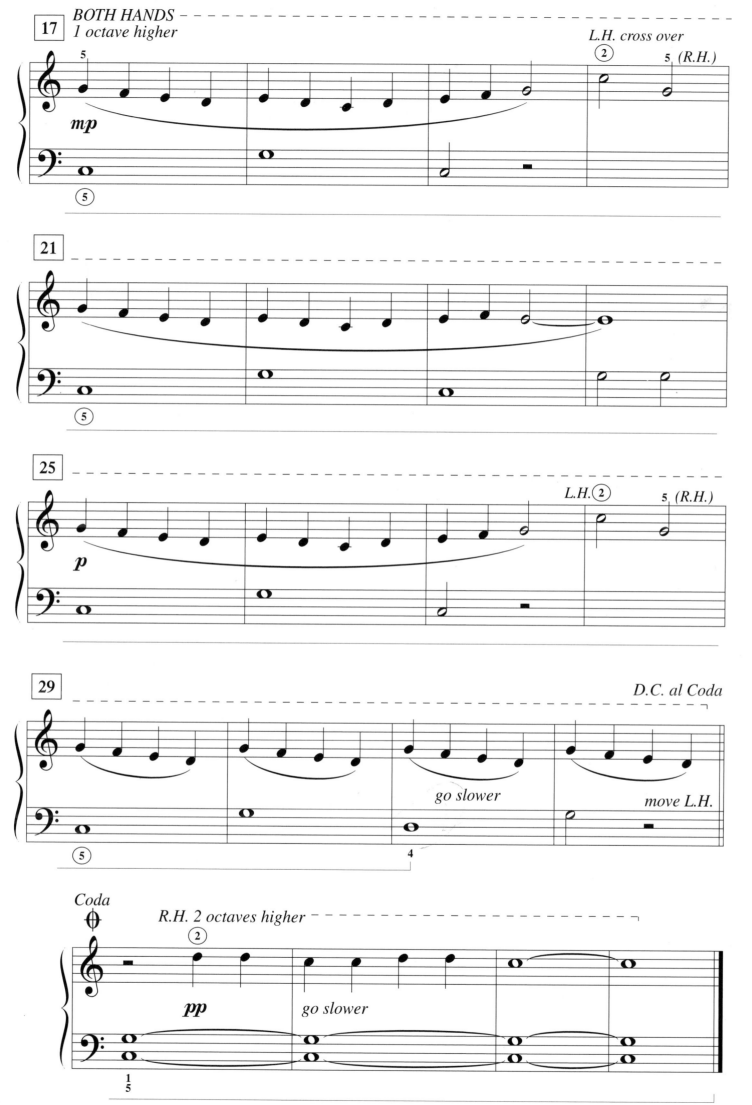

Clowning Around

Imagine a silly clown doing an act full of giggles and wiggles.

L.H. 2 octaves lower - - - ⌐